SECOND GRADE READING FOR KIDS: Reading is Super Fun!

SPEEDY PUBLISHING LLC

Speedy Publishing LLC
40 E. Main St. #1156
Newark, DE 19711
www.speedypublishing.com
Copyright 2015

ISBN: 978-1-6814-5461-0

First Printed 03/04/2015

Contents

ee

cheese
CHēz

Read:

breeze

agree

Write down other examples of ee.

____

____

____

____

ea

clean
klēn

Read:

fear
tear

Write down other examples of ea.

____

____

____

____

oo

school

skо̄оl

Read:

stool

shoot

Write down other examples of oo.

____

____

____

____

OW

snow
snō

Read:

glow
show

Write down other examples of ow.

oa

boat
bōt

Read:

roar
board

Write down other examples of oa.

____

____

____

____

oe

backhoe

ˈbakˌhō

Read:

canoe

cargoes

Write down other examples of oe.

____

____

____

____

ai

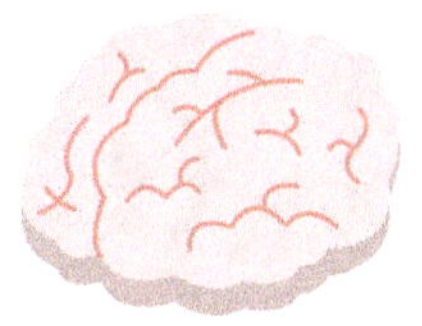

brain
brān

Read:

tail
snail

Write down other examples of ai.

____

____

____

____

ue

blue
blōō

Read:

argue
glue

Write down other examples of ue.

____

____

____

____

br -

brown
broun

bring
brag

Write down other examples of br-.

____

____

____

____

bl -

block
bläk

Read:

blow
bleed

Write down other examples of bl-.

____

____

____

____

cr -

crab
krab

Read:

cry
crayon

Write down other examples of cr-.

____

____

____

____

cl -

cloud
kloud

Read:

clown
clam

Write down other examples of cl-.

____

____

____

____

dr -

drum
drəm

Read:

drag
drown

Write down other examples of dr-.

____

____

____

____

tr -

train
trān

tree
trace

Write down other examples of tr-.

____

____

____

____

fr -

fruit
frо̄оt

Read:

frame

frog

Write down other examples of fr-.

____

____

____

____

fl -

fly
flī

Read:

flew
flag

Write down other examples of fl-.

____

____

____

____

ch -

chain
CHān

Read:

church
chair

Write down other examples of ch-.

____

____

____

____

sh -

shark
SHärk

Read:

shred
shrimp

Write down other examples of sh-.

____

____

____

____

th -

three
THrē

Read:

throw
then

Write down other examples of th-.

____

____

____

____

wh -

wheel
(h)wēl

Read:

when
who

Write down other examples of wh-.

____

____

____

____

- ch

switch
swiCH

Read:

witch
batch

Write down other examples of -ch.

____

____

____

____

- sh

trash
traSH

Read:

brush
hush

Write down other examples of -sh.

____

____

____

____

- th

earth
ərTH

Read:

birth
with

Write down other examples of -th.

____

____

____

____

27

-ck

duck
dək

Read:

rock
black

Write down other examples of -ck.

____

____

____

____

gr -

Read:

grass
gras

grain
grow

Write down other examples of gr-.

____

____

____

____

gl -

glove
gləv

Read:

glow
glam

Write down other examples of gl-.

____

____

____

____

pr -

pretzel
pretsəl

prose

prawn

Write down other examples of pr-.

____

____

____

____

31

pl -

plug
pləg

Read:

plain
plow

Write down other examples of pl-.

____

____

____

____

32

SC -

scale
skāl

Read:

score

scare

Write down other examples of sc-.

____

____

____

____

sk -

skate
skāt

Read:

skew
skate

Write down other examples of sk-.

____

____

____

____

sl -

slipper
ˈslipər

Read:

slam
slide

Write down other examples of sl-.

____

____

____

____

sm -

smock
smäk

Read:

small
smack

Write down other examples of sm-.

____

____

____

____

ph -

photo
ˈfōtō

Read:

phase
pharmacy

Write down other examples of ph-.

____

____

____

____

kn -

knife
nīf

Read:

know
knee

Write down other examples of kn-.

____

____

____

____

qu -

queen
kwēn

Read:

quail
quit

Write down other examples of qu-.

____

____

____

____

wr -

wrench
renCH

Read:

wrong

wrap

Write down other examples of wr-.

____

____

____

____

- tch

watch

wäCH

Read:

batch
hatch

Write down other examples of -tch.

____

____

____

____

- ng

ring
riNG

Read:

bring
wing

Write down other examples of -ng.

____

____

____

____

- ll

ball
bôl

Read:

mall
hall

Write down other examples of -ll.

____

____

____

____

- gh

laugh
laf

rough
tough

Write down other examples of -gh.

____

____

____

____

sn -

snake

snāk

Read:

snap

snack

Write down other examples of sn-.

____

____

____

____

sp -

sponge
spənj

Read:

spike
spoon

Write down other examples of sp-.

____

____

____

____

st -

stone

stōn

Read:

stop
strong

Write down other examples of st-.

____

____

____

____

SW -

swan
swän

Read:

swirl

sweat

Write down other examples of sw-.

____

____

____

____

tw -

twig
twig

twin
twelve

Write down other examples of tw-.

____

____

____

____